"History Is A Part Of Me"

A Hip Hop Poem of African American Inventors

Educational Activity Book

Written By: Shannon Tubbs

Illustration By: Vladimer Cebo

Golden Sky Level Publishing

Noble Writes

Golden Sky Level Publishing
Noble Writes

ISBN-10: 069263212-3
ISBN-13: 978-0-692-63212-3
Printed in the United States of America

History Is A Part Of Me (A Hip Hop Poem of African American Inventors) Educational Activity Book includes an MP3 Download of "I Am Somebody."

Written by: Shannon Tubbs
Illustrated by: Vladimir Cebu

For information regarding special discounts or bulk purchases for schools, churches, etc., please contact: **sales@historyisapartofme.com**.

The author is available for public speaking engagements, workshops, and performances of the song "I Am Somebody" (History is A Part of Me) at: **contact@historyisapartofme.com**.

Website: **Historyisapartofme.com**

Definitions included herein were simplified from Business Directory and Wise Geek.
The Invention dates included in this book are approximate, if not exact. Neither the Author nor Golden Sky Level Publishing assumes claim of copyright in the photographs except for the Limitations on exclusive rights: Fair use (Copyright Law Section 107).

Dear Future Inventors,

I hope that you will stretch your imagination to soar to higher heights. Imagine inventing something totally from scratch or even improving something that has already been created. You could be the first person to introduce a different way of doing things!

When you create, improve, or discover something, you need a patent to protect it. The patent is documentation that proves you are the inventor. Once you have your patent, you can share your invention with the world. Remember to always believe in *you*. It works every time!

Best wishes,
Shannon Tubbs

In • vent (*ihn* vent)

verb

To think up; to create or produce for the first time.

In • ven • tion (*ihn* **ven** *chən*)

noun

Something invented. Especially a new gadget, device, machine, or method; something imagined; the ability or capacity to invent, devise, originate, or imagine; inventiveness, discovery, improvement.

Right (*rite*)

noun

Something that someone could claim that is properly due according to fact or truth; a moral or legal entitlement to have or obtain something or to act in a certain way.

Pat • ent (*pae* *tənt*)

noun

A protected government grant given to an inventor, giving him/her the only right to make, use, or sell an invented device, process, or the like for a specified period of time; to make use, and sell the invention, and to block others from doing so.

Could you imagine what the streets would be like, if there were no traffic lights?

In 1923, **GARRETT A. MORGAN**, figured out something that was very important...

The **TRAFFIC SIGNAL**--so we can safely roll out, making it easier for traffic to flow about.

GARRETT A. MORGAN

Red light, Yellow light, Green light, Go!
GARRETT A. MORGAN, now you know!

GARRETT A. MORGAN

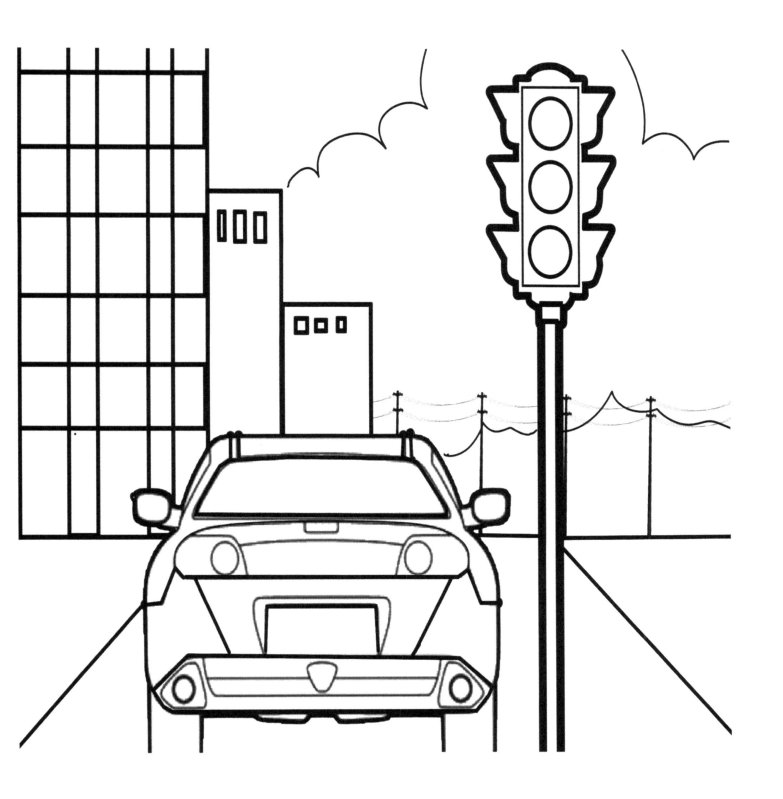

TRAFFIC SIGNAL

If the weather is too hot or a little too cold,
it's all good, a thermometer will let us know.

The temperature tells us if we should wear a coat,
we can turn it up **HIGH**, **OFF**, or down **LOW**.

DAVID CROSTHWAIT, JR.

We can control the degrees by the **THERMOSTAT**.
In 1928, **DAVID CROSTHWAIT, JR.** invented that.

DAVID CROSTHWAIT, JR.

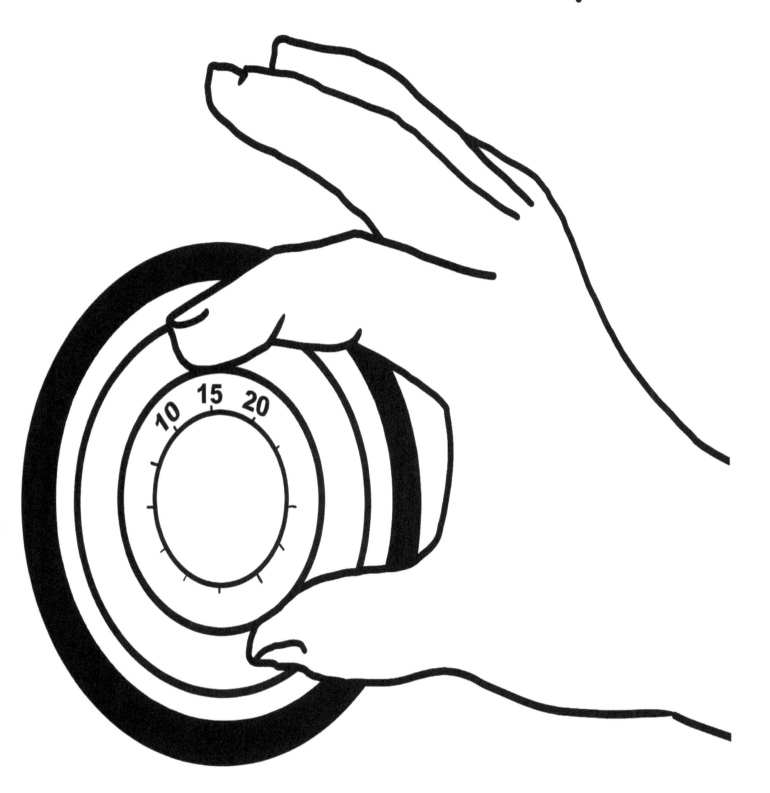

THERMOSTAT

FRED M. JONES was also interested
in the flow of temperature.

He introduced mobile
REFRIGERATORS and **AIR CONDITIONERS!**

FRED M. JONES

Use your imagination,
be brave and create your own road.

You can be whatever you want to be,
and go wherever you want to go!

FRED M. JONES

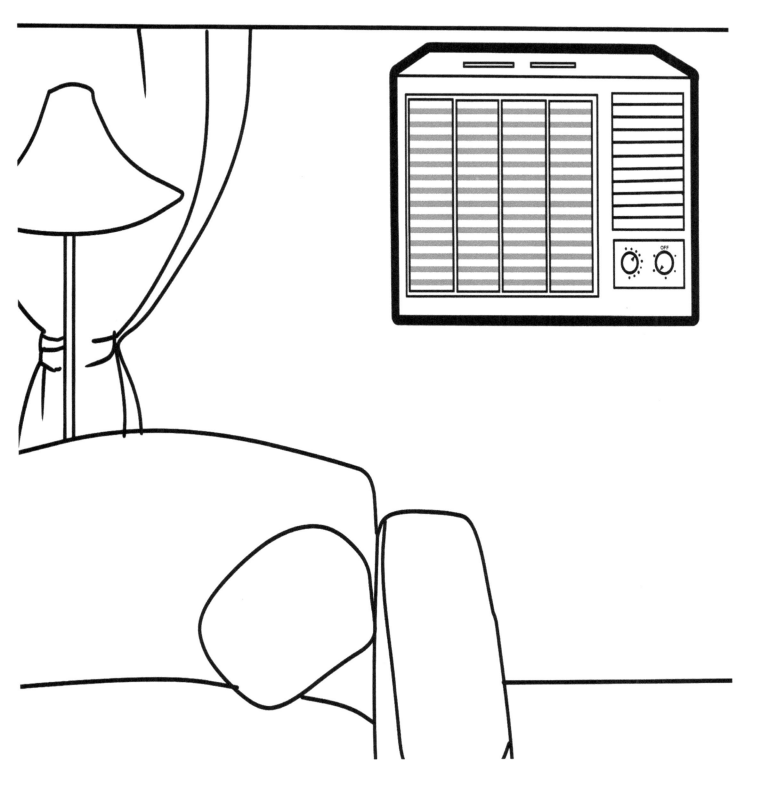

AIR CONDITIONER

Read and write as much as you can,
with a pencil in hand, create a plan.

Sharpen your thoughts by paying attention in school,
think of new ideas with your mind on cruise.

If your pencil is dull, sharpen your tool,
a **PENCIL SHARPENER** is used to make the tip like new!

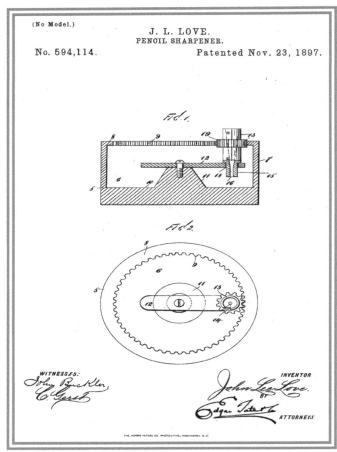

Actual Patent by JOHN LEE LOVE

From what we understand,
in 1897, **JOHN LEE LOVE** came up with that plan.

JOHN LEE LOVE

PENCIL SHARPENER

On September 11, 2001,
there was a lot of damage done.

The World Trade Center was hit and
firefighters had to come.

Where do you think the
FIRE EXTINGUISHER came from?

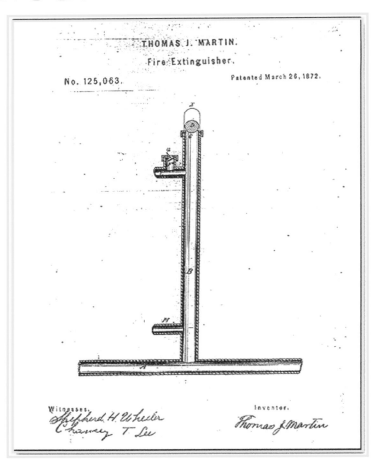

THOMAS J. MARTIN.
Fire Extinguisher.
No. 125,063.   Patented March 26, 1872.

Witnesses,   Inventor,
Shepherd H. Wheeler   Thomas J. Martin
Chauncey T. Lee

Actual Patent by THOMAS J. MARTIN

It was **THOMAS J. MARTIN** in 1872.
Without his idea, what would we do?

THOMAS J. MARTIN

FIRE EXTINGUISHER

Back in the day we had to hang heavy, wet clothes on a rope line outside.

There was no such thing as a
CLOTHES DRYER.

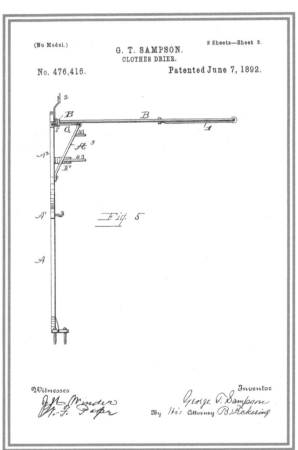

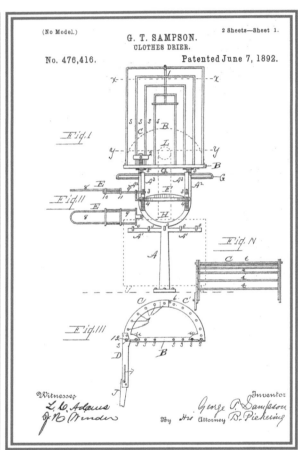

Actual Patents by GEORGE T. SAMPSON

In 1892, **GEORGE T. SAMPSON'S** idea came along, now we can dry clothes inside of our homes!

GEORGE T. SAMPSON

CLOTHES DRYER

ALEXANDER MILES did all of us a favor.
In 1887, he invented the **ELEVATOR**.

ALEXANDER MILES

We don't have to take the stairs in tall buildings
if we don't want to.

The **elevator** can take us safely up or down
to the floor we're going to!

ALEXANDER MILES

ELEVATOR

Long ago there were no ink pens.
People used ink to dip the tip of a bird feather in.

What could be used besides a quill?
Ink inside of the pen, so that it doesn't spill!

WILLIAM B. PURVIS

WILLIAM B. PURVIS, in 18 nine 0,
invented the **FOUNTAIN PEN**--like Whoa!

WILLIAM B. PURVIS

FOUNTAIN PEN

African-American **hair** is curly.
It can be worn short, straight or long.

MADAM CJ WALKER

MADAM CJ WALKER'S invention made
tight curly hair easier to comb.

MADAM CJ WALKER

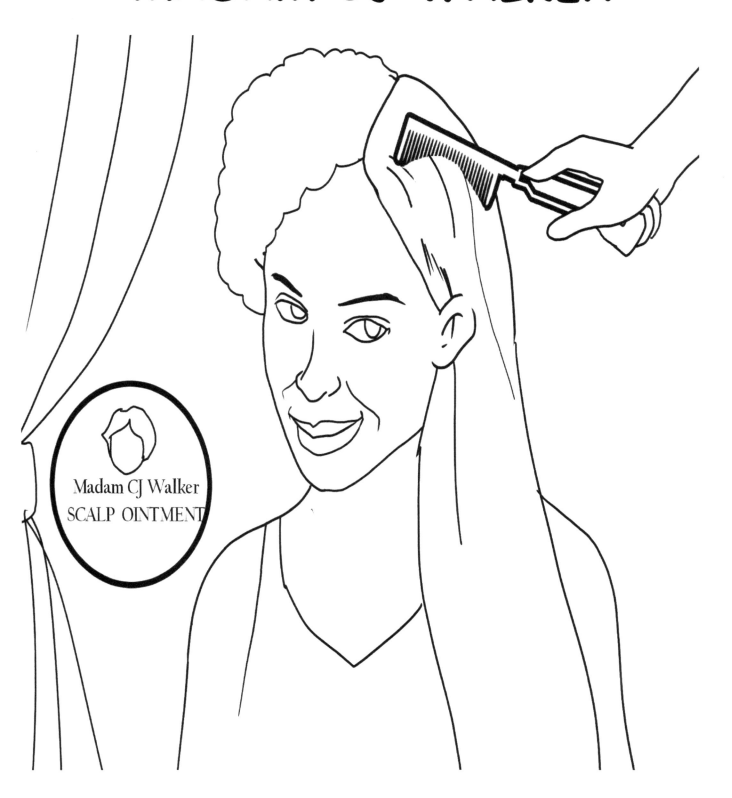

Madam CJ Walker
SCALP OINTMENT

HAIR CARE

PRESIDENT OBAMA worked
hard for the vision that he saw.

The **AFFORDABLE HEALTH CARE LAW**
was invented to give Health Care to all!

PRESIDENT BARACK OBAMA

Hats off to **BARACK**!
He believed in himself and never stopped!

PRESIDENT BARACK OBAMA

"OBAMA CARE"

ACTIVITY PAGES

History IS A PART OF ME

IS A PART OF ME

Name _____ **Date** _____

QUIZ

Circle the correct answer.

1. It is cold inside. What can we do with the ***thermostat***?

    a. We can make the room dark

    b. We can change the temperature

    c. We can make the room shake

2. Why do we need Garrett A. Morgan's ***traffic signal***?

    a. So that bus drivers can see what is behind them

    b. So that truck drivers can honk their horns

    c. For safety so that all drivers can know when to stop or go

3. What should we use to put out a fire?

    a. A broom to sweep the fire away

    b. Ice cubes to cool it down

    c. A fire extinguisher to stop the fire from spreading

4. Did Madam CJ Walker invent the ***pencil sharpener***?

    a. No, Garret Morgan invented the pencil sharpener

    b. Yes, Madam CJ Walker invented the pencil sharpener.

    c. No, Madam CJ Walker invented Hair Care products.

5. Who invented the ***elevator***?

    a. Barack Obama

    b. Alexander Miles

    c. Fred M. Jones

6. Which inventor had an idea about drying clothes?

    a. George Sampson

    b. William Purvis

    c. John Lee Love

Quiz Answers: historyisapartofme.com

IS A PART OF ME

Name _____   Date _____

Hmmm… Thinking of an Invention

Inventors are creative thinkers. They think outside of the box by stretching their imagination. Inventions start out as experiments. Below are some of the thoughts we think the inventors may have had. Name the invention by thinking like an inventor.

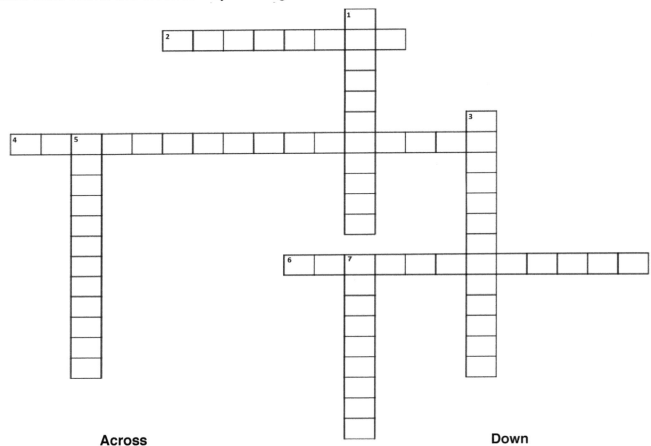

Across

2. Whoa! There are too many floors in the building. What if I couldn't walk up the stairs? How would we get to the top floor safely, if we were in wheel chairs?

4. We need something to stop a fire from burning. Regular water is not enough, of course. Before the fire grows out of control, we need something with force.

6. We wash loads of clothes then we hang them outside. Dang, what if it pours down raining as soon as they have dried? We'll have to wait even longer to bring them inside.

Down

1. I'll just keep it real. Every once in a while, I drop this container of ink and it causes stains when it spills. Is anyone else tired of using a quill?

3. People are driving and no one knows when to stop or when to go. What's up with that? This isn't safe. How can I organize these roads?

5. Some food delivery trucks have air conditioners inside, but that wouldn't stop food from spoiling during a long ride. There has to be another way to keep the food cold. I'm gonna have to work my magic again, with temperature control.

7. Doctor visits can cost a lot of money. Many people have died because they couldn't afford healthcare. "Yes we can" America. It's time for Change everywhere.

Quiz Answers: historyisapartofme.com

IS A PART OF ME

Name _____ **Date** _____

Thinkin' Cap

Look around you. Is there something that you think you may want to invent or improve? Put on your Inventor's Thinkin' Cap. Decide which problem you want to fix. These steps will help:

1. Figure out what could work better or faster. Ask questions. Are you the only one who thinks the problem should be solved? Hopefully not. Write down 3 ideas of new inventions.

    _____

    _____

    _____

2. Draw the Invention that isn't too hard to make. Don't forget to draw how it will look on the inside of your invention. Ask more questions to make sure you are inventing something no one else has thought of yet. Double check by researching online and visiting the Library.

    ┌───┐
    │   │
    │   │
    │   │
    │   │
    │   │
    │   │
    └───┘

3. Write down the things you need to make your invention come to life. If you don't have all of them right now, it's okay you can get them later. When you've finished, protect it. Apply for a Patent at www.uspto.gov. Now you are an Inventor. You can even sell your idea!

    _____

    _____

    _____

The "WHO I AM" Affirmation

I Am Fearless. I Am Able. I Am Willing. I Am Brave.

I Am Grateful for the knowledge of History that was made.

I come from Greatness. I Am Intelligent. I Am Solid as a rock.

I will use my huge imagination to think outside of the box.

I Am different from everyone around me,

like the History that surrounds me.

I choose to believe in myself, even when others doubt me.

I was born with a purpose. I Am not a mistake.

If everything starts with an idea, I have what it takes…

To do great things like those before me,

and to make my future just as proud...

History was a part of me then, and it is happening right now!

Who Am I? I Am Special. I Am History in the making!

-Ms Drama Ganza ©2016

PROOF OF PURCHASE COUPON

History
IS A PART OF ME.com

A HIP HOP POEM OF AFRICAN AMERICAN INVENTORS

Thank you!

FREE MP3 Download of
«I AM SOMEBODY»

Available at
Historyisapartofme.com

Use coupon code:
each1teach1

A Family Collector's Item!

Grow with us! Subscribe to our email list.

Visit: www.historyisapartofme.com

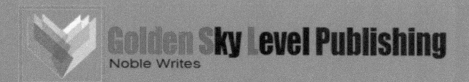

Golden Sky Level Publishing
Noble Writes

About the Author

Shannon (Ms. Drama Ganza) Tubbs is a Hip Hop generation author, songwriter, entertainer, and educator who taught reading to grade school students. Although known for her magnetic stage presence, offstage, Shannon's reserved yet, "get it done" attitude towards supporting and motivating others, is what screams purposeful living. She is a graduate of Musician's Institute in Hollywood, CA and holds Certifications in Music Business-Entrepreneurship, and Leadership Management with an Audio-Video Production Degree.

In addition to songwriting and entertaining, Shannon enjoys spending time with her family, reading, traveling, volunteering, Billiards and people watching. When she is not performing or recording, she finds time for one on one coaching to shed light and insight with peer artists through her online resource imprint, GHT. Passionate about spreading information, *History Is A Part Of Me* workshops/presentations throughout the community "has been the most rewarding in terms of fueling the future".

History is A Part of Me educational coloring book is derived as an updated literary version of her Hip Hop song, **"I Am Somebody."**

CONNECT ONLINE: www.historyisapartofme.com
BOOKING: Contact@historyisapartofme.com

Photo by Michael R. Moore

History
IS A PART OF ME

Schools & Organizations are raving about the "I Am Somebody" music animation and the Educational Activity Book, *History Is A Part Of Me.*

Don't wait! Book the Author for your next workshop or presentation!

contact@historyisapartofme.com

BUY IN BULK!!

Are you interested in purchasing a large quantity?

Visit our website to learn more about bulk ordering and other special offers!

DISCOUNT

MUSIC VIDEO ANIMATION

AAI PACK

T-SHIRT

WWW.HISTORYISAPARTOFME.COM

CPSIA information can be obtained
at www.ICGtesting.com
Printed in the USA
BVHW021501040321
601745BV00009B/335

9 780692 632123